[S.S. 757.]

Ia/55996.

RESULTS OF PRELIMINARY RECONNAISSANCE AND COMPARISON WITH AIR PHOTOGRAPHS OF THE GROUND RE-OCCUPIED IN THE FORWARD AREAS OF THE LYS SALIENT.

GENERAL STAFF (INTELLIGENCE),

GENERAL HEADQUARTERS.

October, 1918.

FireStep Publishing
Gemini House
136-140 Old Shoreham Road
Brighton
BN3 7BD

www.firesteppublishing.com

First published by the General Staff, War Office 1918.
First published in this format by FireStep Editions,
an imprint of FireStep Publishing, in association with
the National Army Museum, 2013.

NATIONAL
ARMY
MUSEUM

www.nam.ac.uk

ISBN 978-1-908487-89-6

Cover design FireStep Publishing
Typeset by FireStep Publishing
Printed and bound in Great Britain

Please note: *In producing in facsimile from original historical documents, any
imperfections may be reproduced and the quality may be lower than modern
typesetting or cartographic standards.*

RESULTS OF PRELIMINARY RECONNAISSANCE AND COMPARISON WITH AIR PHOTOGRAPHS OF THE GROUND RE-OCCUPIED IN THE FORWARD AREAS OF THE LYS SALIENT.

DEFENCES. (Photographs on pages 1—8.)

There had been no systematic trench construction, and where continuous trenches existed they were shallow and had been hastily dug. Defences consisted chiefly of short lengths of trench, rifle pits and machine gun posts.

Considerable trouble had been taken to camouflage these. The parapets were covered with grass and straw, and the trenches themselves with branches, old doors or any other available material. The most successfully concealed were rifle pits, dug-outs, and occupied ditches behind hedges. Signs of activity were visible on photographs chiefly because the dug-outs were so close to the hedge that men had had to pass behind them and thus made a visible track. In many cases, however, it would have been impossible to say whether the hedge concealed rifle pits, dug-outs, or merely ammunition.

DUG-OUTS and SHELTERS. (Photographs on pages 9—24.)

In such continuous trenches as existed, there was practically no dug-out accommodation, but behind reserve positions it was abundant.

Many of the shelters were in the open. A few of them were deep. Others were at the best splinter proof, many being mere bivouacs in shell holes made weather-proof with a roof of boards or corrugated iron, lightly covered with earth and grass.

On good photographs almost all could be detected, but the better ones only by careful examination; it would often be impossible to distinguish the weather-proof shell hole from a camouflaged ammunition one.

MACHINE GUN EMPLACEMENTS. (Photographs on pages 3—8.)

Machine gun emplacements in trenches consisted only of a slight flattening of the parapet, quite impossible to locate on air photographs. They were only noticeable on the ground owing to the proximity of a small splinter proof dug-out and empty cartridge cases. Examples of machine gun emplacements in the open are shown.

Note.—No trench mortar emplacements were seen, but from the ammunition found it appears probable that medium and heavy trench mortars were fired from ruined houses and shell holes.

AMMUNITION DUMPS. (Photographs on pages 25—28.)

The whole forward area may be said to have been one vast scattered dump. Ammunition was stored in houses, in shell holes, under hedges and banks, in ditches, on the roadside and in the open.

Lying uncamouflaged on open ground, ammunition, if in sufficiently small quantities (about 10 to 20 shells according to size), is quite invisible on any but the best photographs.

Behind hedges or crumbled walls, preferably on the north side, it can be dumped in considerable quantities and will remain invisible, provided that signs of activity do not betray it. In such positions, it was often found covered with vegetation or branches, with good results.

PRINTED IN FRANCE BY ARMY PRINTING AND STATIONERY SERVICES   PRESS A--1/19—8102S—250.

In the case of shell hole dumps, a really good large scale photograph will always show that a shell hole is not empty; on the ordinarily clear photograph at our disposal this can, as often as not, be determined by careful examination. Signs of activity are also generally to be seen.

In several places, ammunition was found in shell holes close to those tracks which had been attributed to caterpillar tractors or tank autos, but which were actually made by heavy wagons. Where these tracks are seen, the ground should be carefully searched for ammunition. A good stereo is often helpful in locating this form of dump.

Shells dumped in small cuttings in a bank can only be located by spoil being left about or by signs of activity.

By far the most effective method, except perhaps the use of ruined houses, is to dump ammunition along the side of a road which has the shelter of hedges or trees. The road obviates all the difficulty of tracks, and the ammunition itself, even in quite large quantities, cannot be seen on photographs.

The difficulty of detecting ammunition dumped in these ways is further increased by the fact that, from the appearance of the object on the photograph, it is generally impossible to say whether activity behind a hedge or bank denotes ammunition or camouflaged rifle pits or dug-outs; or, again, to say whether a covered shell hole contains ammunition or merely shelter room for personnel.

This fact should be noted and might be turned to account.

CONCRETE. (Photograph on page 29.)

The enemy's withdrawal apparently interrupted preparations for the extensive use of concrete shelters in houses. Only two or three completed examples, however, were found. They were of medium strength with only some 2 feet of reinforced concrete, and the appearance of the house was as little altered as possible. Photographs show nothing to make the presence of concrete suspected, nor would they be likely to do so, at any rate until the house had been shelled.

CAMOUFLAGE.

It is abundantly clear that camouflage is best employed in completing natural protection which is already good, and also that, however good the camouflage may be, signs of activity must be avoided if it is to be entirely successful.

One instance is very instructive. There was one gun pit which remained undetected from photographs, although it had been located by sound rangers and flash spotters. It was close to a road (there were consequently no tracks), and the red and white camouflage extended from broken masonry of the same colour. A companion pit, equally well camouflaged but farther from the road, was given away by tracks and engaged for destruction.

B dug-out on page 19 is also interesting. The short track from the road to the entrance is practically hidden by a bush on either side of it, and the roof is sloped downwards away from the bushes so that the strongest shadow thrown would fall near the bushes and might pass unnoticed. This dug-out was camouflaged with dead clover stalks and should be compared with C (on the same photograph), where the straw used has only served to make it more obvious.

One fact should not be lost sight of, namely, that almost all these camouflaged defences, dug-outs and dumps were practically invisible from the ground until one was within a very few yards of them. In some cases, they might have been walked over before being noticed.

GENERAL STAFF (INTELLIGENCE),
 GENERAL HEADQUARTERS,
  October, 1918.

1.
Short Lengths of Camouflaged Trench.

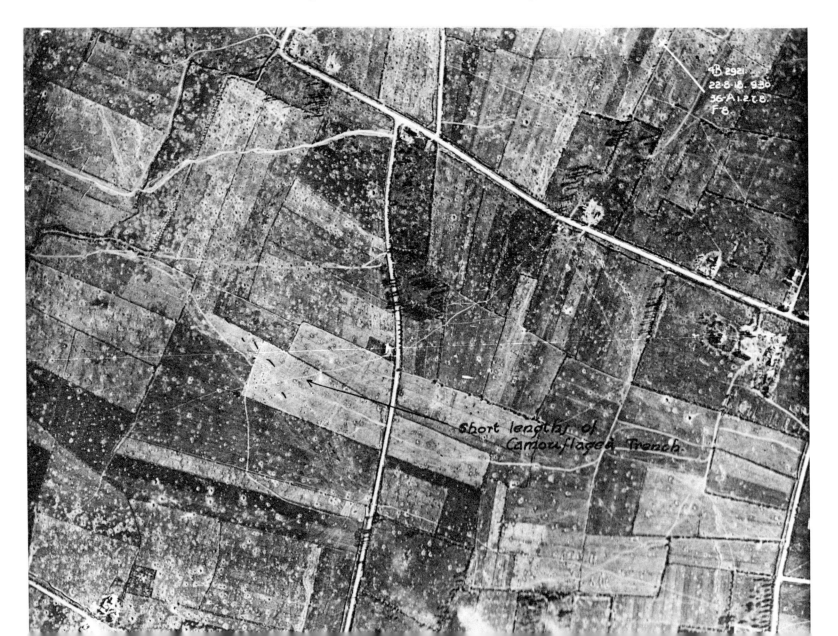

Short lengths of
Camouflaged Trench

2.
Short Lengths of Camouflaged Trench.

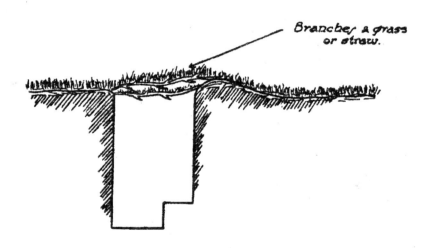

Branches & grass
or straw.

3.
Heavy Machine Gun Posts :
also Rifle Pits behind Hedges.

4.
Heavy Machine Gun Posts.

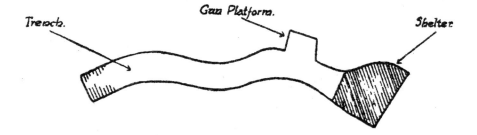

5.
Machine Gun Post as Defence to Battery

See ground photographs on pages 7 & 8.

6.
Line of Machine Gun and Infantry Posts in Organized Shell Holes.

7.
Machine Gun Post (see page 5).

■Front View

8.
Machine Gun Post (see page 5).

Back View

9.
Line of Camouflaged Pits behind Hedge also Dug-Outs in Bank.

See ground photographs

10.
Line of Camouflaged Pits behind Hedge
(see A on page 9).

A.

11.
Line of Camouflaged Pits behind Hedge
(see B on page 9).

12.
Line of Camouflaged Pits behind Hedge
(see B on page 9).

13.
Dug-Outs (see C on page 9).

C.

14.
Dug-Out (see C on page 9).

15.
Mined Dug-Outs.

Mined Dug-outs
camouflaged.

16.
Mined Dug-Out.

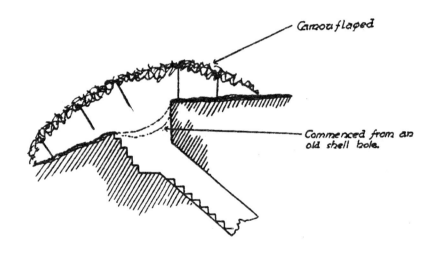

Camouflaged

Commenced from an
old shell hole.

17.
Dug-Outs.

18.
Dug-Out.

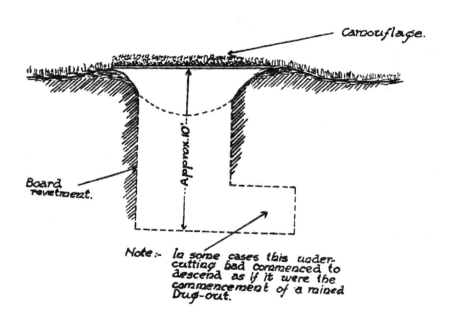

Camouflage.

Approx. 10'.

Board revetment.

Note :- In some cases this under-cutting had commenced to descend as if it were the commencement of a mined Dug-out.

19.
Dug-Outs.

20.

Dug-Out (see A on page 19).

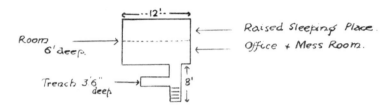

Room 6' deep.
Trench 3'6" deep.
12'
Raised Sleeping Place.
Office + Mess Room.
8'

21.
Dug-Out (see B page 19).

B.

A Front View

22.
Dug-Out (see B on page 19).

Back View

B.

23.
Weather-Proof Shell Holes.

24.
Weather-Proof Shell Hole Bivouac.

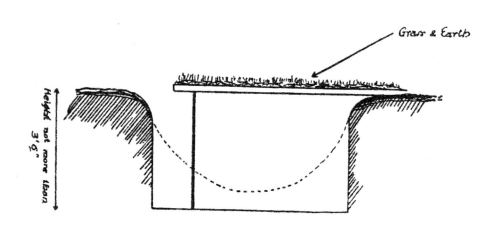

25.
Ammunition in Shell Holes.

26.
Ammunition in Shell Holes.

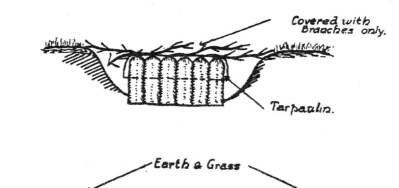

Covered with Branches only.

Tarpaulin.

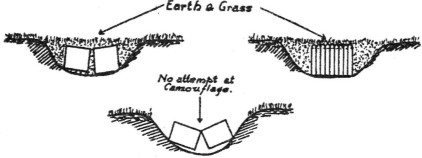

Earth & Grass

No attempt at Camouflage.

27.
Ammunition in Shell Holes and behind Hedges.

28.
Ammunition given away by Heavy Wagon Tracks.

29.
Concreted House.